Lullaby for the Grieving

Also by Ashley M. Jones

Magic City Gospel
dark // thing
Reparations Now!

Lullaby *for the* Grieving

Ashley M. Jones

HUB CITY PRESS
SPARTANBURG, SC

Executive Director, Publisher: Meg Reid
Managing Editor: Kate McMullen
Marketing Assistant: Julie Jarema
Editor: Katherine Webb-Hehn
Proofreader: Stephanie Trott

Book Design: Kate McMullen
Cover image courtesy of Ashley M. Jones
Author Photo: Ashley M. Jones

Type: Adobe Caslon Pro
Display: Naiche

Library of Congress Cataloging-in-Publication Data

Names: Jones, Ashley M., 1990- author.
Title: Lullaby for the grieving / Ashley M. Jones.
Other titles: Lullaby for the grieving (Compilation)
Description: Spartanburg, SC : Hub City Press, 2025.
Identifiers: LCCN 2025018300 (print)
LCCN 2025018301 (ebook)
ISBN 9798885740586 (paperback)
ISBN 9798885740623 (epub)
Subjects: LCGFT: Poetry. Classification:
LCC PS3610.O595 L85 2025 (print)
LCC PS3610.O595 (ebook)
DDC 811/.6—dc23/eng/20250509
LC record available at
https://lccn.loc.gov/2025018300
LC ebook record available at
https://lccn.loc.gov/2025018301

City of SPARTANBURG south carolina

HUB CITY PRESS
153 N Spring Street
Spartanburg, SC 29306
864.577.9349 | www.hubcity.org

for Dad, our angel

for every broken heart

Table *of* Contents

What It Really Is 1

I feel powerful when 2

Home: Variations 4

Grief Interlude 6

All God's Children Got Wings 7

A Meat and Three for the Jubilee 9

The Heart 13

Freedom Sermon—Alabama, USA 15

A Map of the Capitol—Montgomery, AL, USA 16

When You Ask Me From Where My Help Comes 18

In the Beginning, There Was the Word 20

Grief Interlude II 22

Love Poem 23

I Think of You, Alabama 24

Black, Black Blue 25

A Portrait of Harriet 26

Grief Interlude III 30

A Lesson in Distraction / Abstraction—2020 Time Capsule 31

On My Way to the Edmund Pettus Bridge,
I Think of My Father 33

Wellness Exam 34

African American Literature I 36

Conflict // War 37

38 Watcher Woman, or, Upon Seeing a Grown White Man Look a Black Girl Up and Down as she Passsed By on a Birmingham Street
40 Masks
42 Grief Pantoum
43 *Grief Interlude IV*
44 It All Begins Here
45 I Know I Feel It, But If I Told You That
46 *Grief Interlude V*
47 Ida Mae, Queen of Joy
48 *Grief Interlude VI*
49 Lullaby for the Grieving
50 Grief
51 Love and Happiness
52 *Grief Interlude VII*
53 On Entering the New Year Without My Father
54 Snow Poem
63 Imagine Us, In Love with the World

67 Acknowledgements

What It Really Is

an american acrostic

Coastline broke into forest into village, seas
rolled in uninterrupted waves. Somewhere,
I insisted on being born. Somewhere, countless
tribes called each other by name. Somewhere, a black panther
inches ever closer to its prey. Somewhere, the sun is a halo.
Cameroon is a whisper in my blood—the ancestry kit tells me
as it uses DNA to glue me back together. Can it catch
long strands of lineage shucked and punched to pulp? Somewhere, a clot

rubs its rigid way into my veins. It calls itself america.
And the seas were parted with my body over and over.
Centuries are cut into the skin stretched across my womb. Will
every lifted voice be silenced? When does a

theory become a threat? I return to the coastline. Village. Bright arc,
halo of sun. All this has been bloodied. Even my body, a wound, infinitely.
Earth spins on an unfair axis. Streets curdle. Again, blood.
O, come back coastline. Come back, un-shipped sea.
Remember the way my people were robbed of bone and breath?
You called it liberty.

I feel powerful when

my hair comes out just like I pictured it: full fro, twists, braids, a shimmering mass of kink / I sing all the words to "Reasons" by Earth, Wind, and Fire, and I even hit some of the notes so beautifully, don't you agree / it's summertime and my legs are shined up in the way Black legs shine, soaking up light, space, time, your attention and wonder / I laugh without stopping—when my laugh makes my mom laugh, too. When her face ignites—

when I'm BlackBlack Black Black Black Black Black Black Black Black Black Black Black Black Black Black

Black Black Black Black Black Black Black Black Black
Black Black Black Black Black Black Black Black Black
Black Black Black Black Black Black Black Black Black
Black Black Black Black Black Black Black Black Black
Black Black Black Black Black Black Black Black Black
Black Black Black Black Black Black Black Black Black
Black Black Black Black Black Black Black Black Black
Black Black Black Black Black Black Black Black Black
Black Black Black Black Black Black Black Black Black
Black Black Black Black Black Black Black BlackBlack
Black Black Black Black Black Black Black Black Black
Black Black Black Black Black Black Black Black Black
Black Black Black Black Black Black Black Black Black
Black Black Black Black Black Black Black Black Black
Black Black Black Black Black Black Black Black Black
Black Black Black Black Black Black Black Black Black
Black Black Black Black Black Black Black Black Black
Black Black Black Black Black Black Black Black Black
Black Black Black Black Black Black Black Black Black
Black Black Black Black Black Black Black Black Black
Black Black Black Black Black Black Black Black Black
Black Black Black BlackBlack Black Black Black Black
Black Black Black Black Black Black Black Black Black
Black Black Black Black—

Home: Variations

After Carrie Mae Weems

Start here. Once you cross the threshold, you're home. The door
is what brings you from *out* to *in*. The door:

the only unit of measurement, not how "poor,"
not four walls, not foundation or drywall or chimney or roof. A door

opens a place into home. Remember, on Gooree
Island, they walked us through that unknown mouth, the Door

Of No Return? Remember how we, unmoored,
made our own bodies a home, made doorways

out of our voices in the air, their undeniable treasure.
The homes we make of touch, how we adore

each other. How a nod can mean *you're home*—home in feet planted, freely, on the floor.
My grandmothers made homes out of things that were not houses—the fervor

of their Blackmother spirits filling the Bessemer projects, the Greensboro trailer—
no fireplace but the warm tv set, no yard but the red clay. The splendor

of what lives beyond what you call *welfare, inner city, blight.* Don't you know our
words are a way home? We even bend language into a liberating door.

I used to think my proper tongue meant I leaned toward
the thing that stole our culture. But we can't outgrow our home. Or,

we have never left in the ways that matter—home in our flavors,
our dances, the languages we *live*. Home is in us, behind a locked door.

We bent the blue cries of this place into full bodied song, bent frail walls into shelter.
We bent the cast off portions into a meal, we bent two cents into a dollar.

We bent redlines and tenements into a sanctuary you can't enter.
Want to know how Black folks find our way back to Heaven? Start here. Open the door.

Grief Interlude

I question the air. The spaces between the leaves. The sound of water. Has summer always been this hot, this blue? Where are you in this reality? Where did you go? Seems one day you were standing right in front of me, holding the door, loading my weekend bag into the trunk, saying goodbye and lingering, a moon in orbit. Did you know? There was something in the corners of your eyes, yes, but was it the gray of last breaths? Was it your own heartbeat telling you it was tired? I want to feel human again. Now, a shell of flesh in the wind. Where did you go? Were you here?

All God's Children Got Wings

> I got wings, you got wings, all of God's children got wings! When I get to Heaven gonna put on my wings; I'm gonna fly all over God's Heaven! Heaven, Heaven. Everybody talkin' 'bout Heaven ain't goin' there, Heaven, Heaven; gonna fly all over God's Heaven!
>
> Lyrics from the Negro Spiritual

> They brought me away with two of my children, and would'nt let me see my husband—they did'nt sell my husband, and I did'nt want to go;—I was so confus'd and 'istratcted, that I did'nt know hardly what I was about—but I did'nt want to go, and I jumped out of the window.
>
> Ann Williams, who jumped out of a third story tavern window to protest being sold away from her children and into the Deep South, 1815

when I was born, God gave me wings—
feathers fit to fly—
the wide breadth of the open sky—

when I was born, God said *you are* and I was.
this place called maryland can't own my flesh.
this place called america can't own my blood.
no master over my love or my womb—no master
no man making devil's deals
no mistress holding her skin above mine
no five flat dollars enough to sell me.

they say I'm going south—
they can't take us from Africa anymore
so they'll just take us from here:
can the capitol's shadow hide this sin?
in the south, the sun is mad just like we are—
it burns the whole land
to spite the men who make us work it.
it reminds us that something in this world can be warm.
my children are traded for vulgar currency.

and I remember God said *you are made of wings*,
and then I remember the sky, its gift,
those clouds which they cannot hold, and my soul—
I remember that God does not know their names.
no slavemaster will see the pearly gates.
and the window, it says, *you are*.
it says I got wings. Feathers fit to fly.
when I get to Heaven—there'll be no bones to break,
no families unglued by the spit of satan—
I'm gonna fly all over God's Heaven.
I'm gonna fly.

A Meat and Three for the Jubilee

With thanks to JBT

i. candiedyams

mama, sweet as the fresh scent of new clean laundry. sweet as a curl unraveled from a pink foam roller on a fresh press. sweet like her mama taught her to be, her mama who knew what it meant to raise a child you didn't carry in your own womb. her mama who could make yams like no one else on this dull planet—who could make sugar out of laughs alone, who could cut the yams up and cook them bright and orange. could blend them up and make a pie every thanksgiving and christmas—see how the nutmeg floats its spice, see how you can slice it up when it's just a little bit warm—faint memory of the oven still lingering, see how it stays intact in your own eager hand? crust as strong as a mama. no, stronger—a black mama—strong, and it knows when to give, when to fold around the soft filling, the soft you, the soft black baby and hold—

II. Hoppin John: A Blues

after Tyehimba Jess

she's got some eyes—bette davis, no, black—
on our plates, she shimmies between the rice
and makes a lucky meal where there is lack—
not lima, pinto, just blackeyes suffice.

what alchemy where peas become pennies,
where even here we can be rich with pork,
this meal is tender medicine, ready
to heal what keeps us broken, to unyoke

ourselves away from helpless and enslaved.
we slice we sear we simmer and we braise
we hunt we chop we pick we stand amazed,
we serve it up and then we offer praise

the white blending around it—a whole note
supple with salt and onion and butter
this marriage on our Sunday plate, we float—
this here's a john that hops like no other.

the currency we want is born of soil,
stewed and heaped while the crops break for winter.
when we need fresh warm hope, brought to the boil,
so we're not chained to ruin, we splinter

and we build ourselves a future, we cook
it down until it's soft enough to eat,
we count our blessings, count the faith it took
to be here, to have vegetables and meat.

blackeyed peas and white rice on new year's day,
we pray this meal will keep the doom away—

III. Greens&Bread

the soil remembers the names of our mothers
                                                            our fathers
                                                            even the babies who
made their first and last milkbreath and went to heaven. greens
grow from even the dead-full soil.

greens stretch their velvet shoulders and ruffle in the south.
they bend their backs to let us wash their spines.
they remember us remembering,
remember plucking them from your father's raised bed?
remember how he taught you which ones to keep
and which ones to throw back to feed the soil anew?
remember beholding their beauty at the sink,
the way veins shined through even in the pot
gleaming with bacon fat,
even in the soup of stock and water
as it pulls softness from their mouths?

and the bread—how incomplete they are without it,
cornmeal raising up to meet buttermilk, to meet egg,
to meet the hot glaze of oil in the cast iron,
the crack of the crust a guarantee.

the pot liquor is a broth of memory. greens remember it all.
and on the plate, remember how the bread acculturates to let its
unctuous river in? softened, yes, but not weak,
crumbling, instead, toward a new identity.
and our forks and our fingers gobble it up.

IV. Freefriedfowl At The Coon Chicken Inn

> Stop talking about the South. As long as you South of the Canadian border, you South.
>
> el Hajj Malik el Shabazz, FKA Malcolm X

brother malcolm told us anything below canada was dixie—
so here we are at your red open mouth
in salt lake city,
in seattle,
in portland—
not as hot as alabama, but inferno all the same.

here, where we see our faces through an unkind mirror,
a funhouse of minstrel men and unending smiles—
we no marketing ploy, we no shiny commercial coon,
we won't open our teeth for you to walk through.

oh, you think me a novelty?
you think I was born to whistle all the cotton tunes
and serve your dinner piping hot?
you think this grease dripping from my gums,
you think this tongue made of watermelon,
you think this body full of belly rubbing
but no,
what you see are my people opening into a scream.
your fine breaded chickens,
coming home to roost.

The Heart

> Make us worthy, God in Heaven / of this goodly land of Thine.
>
> Alabama State Song

Dixie is a body, and we are the heart of it.

And because a body must breathe, we have filled the air
with fruit and grain and song. We have lined our lungs in cotton.
And because hearts must have blood,
we plucked it and it spread
in stripes and in crosses on our flags,
in a bruise of red and blue.

We, the heart, make wartime music—a drumming sound
which calls our steps out of the dirt.

God pulled us all from that same dirt—
our bones know the earth's first anthems,
and those melodies fortify us.
Alabama—an innate melody.

This heart has history—
see the way the stars line up our sky?
They map each vein,
vessels in the pumping whole:
the cradle built in 1861,
the bomb of 1963,
the outcry reaching Washington,
Shuttlesworth, made of steel,
a city built by magic,
the jails bursting with fighters and freedoms
and *why we can't wait*—

Dixie is a body. We, heart-shaped
and making life, branch,
river and engine.
We make this a good
and worthy place.

Freedom Sermon—Alabama, USA

Why do we want to kill all the broken people? What is wrong with us, that we think a thing like that can be right?
Bryan Stevenson

You are a light. You are the light.
John Lewis

The chickens knew. Their blood in the soil knew
when it spilled, when it curdled in the pan
that there was a movement brewing in you,
John, they heard you speak God's word—the right man
for the job, by far. The chickens knew, yes,
but so did the Bull, the hose, sweet Dixie
and the US President, too. Oh, Bless.
Blessèd freedom fighters who unfix the
chains and prison bars—stripes rough and unjust
on a flag sewn with blood. Bryan, when did
you learn that dollars grease the system's rust
and fill the cells to bursting? God forbid
the least of us unite. Now, we must fight—
the thing you cannot bury is the light.

A Map of the Capitol—Montgomery, AL, USA

For one hundred thirty-one years, a street in Montgomery was named after Jefferson Davis, the first president of the Confederacy.

For thirty five years, Jefferson Davis Avenue was a cross street of Rosa Parks Avenue.

In 2021, Jefferson Davis Avenue was renamed Fred Gray Avenue.

In 2021, I became the first person of color and youngest person to serve as Poet Laureate of Alabama. The Office of the Poet Laureate in Alabama has existed since 1930.

jefferson davis
cradled the confederates
in montgomery

in montgomery
a street can hold a cradle
and an auction block

in montgomery
some babies are sold, while some
can be president

eight presidents, not
confederate presidents,
owned slaves while they served

jefferson davis
was a cotton man—his fields
stretched mississippi

in montgomery
in the old house chamber,
the halls lined with men

who mastered this state
until it bled with black pain;
the old house chamber

hoists a monument
to its heritage of hate—
no nuance in secession,

no way to wrestle
free of its loud, red siren
yelling through all time—

in montgomery
i was a Black First, watched by
my family, friends,

by alabama,
by ghosts of jeff davis'
red states and armies,

by dead auctioneers
& the angels up for sale,
by false memory.

i heard them all speak,
heard the streets scream all at once,
and yes, i listened—

the sharp traffic of
so many intersections,
and my voice cut through

rosa parks boarded
at court square to ride a bus
home from work to rest

rosa parks boarded
at court square. the auction block's
ghost beneath her feet

rosa parks boarded—
and claudette colvin boarded—
remember them both

name the street rosa
but jeff davis oversees—
plantation highway

what intersection
splits patriot and rebel?
i often wonder

we dedicate streets
to ghosts—their storied flesh blares
bright red, blood white, blue

When You Ask Me From Where My Help Comes

My help comes from the Lord.
Psalm 121

God is God / is God.
Faisal Mohyuddin

the face of God was shown to my people
in the dark and vast nighttime sky
in a town just like this one some four centuries ago.
it does not matter where in this country you are.
my people were there, and they searched
for God
who they knew before the sin of those ships.
God is God no matter the continent.

the stars are windows to heaven—
we can follow them to glory, and so can you.
do you think the face of God is a human face?
how can something as big, as world-making,
as ocean-building, as mountain-moving,
as look-how-this-earth-knows-to-keep-spinning,
be contained by such inconsequential instruments as skin and bones?

God wears many faces, all of them you and all of them me,
all of them all of us, always. a face as singular
and as varied as all the spears of grass
making a whole holy green.

it's true, my people saw the face of God
and it looked like the cool river opening up to welcome their feet,
to erase their scent as they were hunted
by people who maybe were our great great great grandfathers and their sons,
by the dogs which did nothing but what they were told.
the face of God in the sunlight warming the backs of ants
as they build their hallways made of earth,
grain by grain. the face of God in the owl's haunt,
in the space between our palms as they meet in prayer.

the face of God in our prayers—in the breath
on our anxious and grateful lips,
in the many names by which we call God,
in all the languages made for us to speak.
God in truth, unmitigated, painful, and real.
God sees us now. What will we show Him?

In the Beginning, There Was the Word

for Joe Minter and the African Village in America

And when those white-sailed ships
piled us together, cargo in the hull of hell,
the word rode with us. Our tongues
anointed with the power of God.
When the lash found our language,
when they said don't read or write,
our tongues were still gilded with a heavenly word.
We still sang that holy song,
even in this strange land. Even here, God spoke
to us and through us.
Our hands made language
and earth became fruitful,
and song became prayer,
and a people made do
with the bones and scraps of america.

And we became messengers
with each sin pitched against us—
in Birmingham, there was God
in the feet of the marchers
and in the starched collar of Fred Shuttlesworth,
in the curls and dimples
of those four girls,
in the boyish joy of Virgil and Johnnie
before their song was cut short.

Messengers, all of us, speaking the word
God left us in this weary land.
Messengers with the word as their spear,
messengers speaking life into each brick,
each crop, each stitch, each book we made.
And there is a messenger on Nassau Avenue
with the word clear and strong on his tongue.

A warrior for the Lord, a servant of the word.
And the ancestors find his brown hands
and anoint them, and metal becomes message,
wood and paint interpret scripture,
the wind blows through, and there is God.

In the beginning there was the word,
and the word remains.
We are a living tongue—
the word is a torch and we tote it proudly,
what you hear is our collective soul,
what you see is love walking, God's blueprint,
ours is an unstoppable song.

Grief Interlude II

I want to see the curve of your legs moving strong down the Birmingham streets. The shine of your fireman's badge. The scratch of your cough in the morning. Even the slurp of your coffee, of your teeth against your toothpick that made my skin crawl. I want the way you'd mess my hair even though I am a Black woman and we hate that. I want the way your eyes turned boyish when you were happy. Or when you were sad. I want the way you'd carry my luggage every single time it needed carrying. The way, sometimes, you'd even reach for my adult hand crossing the street. I want the safety of girlhood. I want your breath, opening against the new day.

Love Poem

the space you leave on the couch beside me
anytime you get up, the snores we scratch
into each other's sleep, the way you read
everything, always. the way you know much
more than I ever will. the many days
we spent living twelve hard hours apart—
you in your Subaru, the flights I braved.
the way I thought no one could hold my heart.
even the fear stretched between us back then,
that, too, makes the shape of us. of the love
I hope remains. or, that won't be written
in my catalog of pain. that above
all, even if we do or do not last,
I want to think fondly of us, our past.

I Think of You, Alabama

at the World Games

Alabama, you are the yellowhammer's song,
the trill of its bright welcome,
its wings, a fluttering harmony.
Alabama, they say stars fell here
and it's true—look at the dew making glitter
over the fields,
look at the twinkles
shaking out of our cackles and smiles,
the stars in our glasses, cooling our sweet tea.

When I think of love
I think of you, Alabama—
the way you defy the harsh touch of man
and bloom anyway.
You rise up around your people
and you show them strong and sparkling
against any shadow, any chain.
The sun breaks from its moontime bud
and petals into light over you, Alabama,
blessing the morning, red in its glow.

When I think of love, Alabama,
I think of the children,
all of them exactly as they are,
whoever they are.
They know what it means to be free,
they show me that our history can embolden us
and move us forward. It can steel us as we march.
They imagine a future, Alabama,
and it's coming, the freshest crop,
our most sacred harvest.
May our hands be ready to pluck it,
let them be clean enough to hold it close.

Black, Black Blue

after Erin Leann Mitchell

—this tale begins before the first ship
stole wind in its poisonous sails—

our hands, blue as ocean
and strong as it, too,
twisting our memories,
our history into braids—
our regal ancestry moisturizing
even our tightest curls—
the nobility of nappy,
the Blue Magic brilliance under our bonnets—
what a path even our hair can weave,
and no,
you can't follow—

our feet hold a kind of knowledge
only God knows—
ten toes, each one
its own commandment—
our feet, how they carry us,
move us through all this world's
sludge of blood and money
and fly us to our dreams—the wildest
the farthest,
the biggest,
the blackest,

and running, running, breathing in our glorious skin—

we are eternally
unkillably
phenomenally
alive.

A Portrait of Harriet

with thanks to Dr. Rebekah Griffin Greene, who set these words to music.

I. Hymn For Harriet's Hands

Praise the palms.
Did they hold your babies' cheeks
and calm their weeping? Did they rise
to meet the crater opened in your skull,
did they touch the blood
and feel God pulsing there, loud and looming?
Did they make the shape of prayer, face to face?

Praise the fingers
and their ten-fold nimble army,
their *look* as you reached toward freedom,
their *stop* when danger blared ahead,
their *quiet* as you gripped
the knowing pistol, it's warning,
if you hold us back—

And praise the skin, its ripple
over the back of each wide knuckle.
Its gentle glisten—
the sweetening of sunrise
making soft your readied fists,
the fight of them a blessing
ever ready to explode.

II. Harriet, The Locomotive

freedomfreedomfreedomfreedomfreedomfreedom

the train was made of flesh
the train was made of blood
the train, built by Jesus himself,
and Harriet saw it plain—

freedomfreedomfreedomfreedomfreedomfreedom

it was a train through the woods,
fueled by feet alone. fueled by hope alone.
fueled by the visions God kept blowing,
like fire, in Harriet's eyes.
the fire said *go* and she followed it,
the fire said *run* and she did,
and the fire said *freedom*
and she willed herself free.
and she held that fire in her two hands
and opened her palms to those still lost
in captivity and they followed, and they ran,
and they knew it was God speaking, too.
and they knew the long, lonely way
would blossom into Glory—

into *freedomfreedomfreedomfreedomfreedomfreedom*

IV. These Feet Can Dance, Too

my feet were born to move.
born to feel the earth
and all its rocks and ridges
to spell God's name over and again
with my soles. my soul
is tied to this land
and it pulls me north, it pulls me out of chains
and into the stars, the night, which is a kind of earth.
the night which covers me, pulls me forward,
hides me from the men who want to tie my soul down.
the men who want it stuck here in this hell.

my feet were born to dance, too—
what else can I call this journey toward my freedom
but a waltz set to heavenly music,
but a promise made to my body when it was formed by God?
but a guarantee if I can keep the faith—

my feet, they run this country a hundred times over.
the dirt is laced with my blood,
my blood, from sea to shining sea,
my blood, across state lines, across county lines,
across the lie of these lines making evil territories.
my blood draws a new map. my blood remakes the world.

my feet were born to move
and they'll move and keep on moving.
every single love I have will be taken on to freedom.
step by holy step.

V. HOLYHEADHARRIET

the eye of God is planted between my brow the eye of God is opening at the top of my head the eye of God was made with blood, was made from the hands of an ungodly master the eye of God pierced my head in two the eye of God said look and I saw it the eye of God showed me rivers and fields and trees that would shelter me on my way the eye of God told me I would not be enslaved the eye of God showed me all the shades of my humanity showed me how to see my people my people my people are the eye of God, too my people bloom from my brow my people are the top of my head and the soles of my feet my people are made with blood my people are hurting at the hands of an ungodly master my people have pierced me in two my people said look and I saw them my people showed me their blood in the rivers my people showed me their blood in the fields my people showed me their bodies in the trees and the shelter I could make for them on my way my people told me they were not enslaved my people showed me all the shades of my humanity my people showed me how to see my people how to see my God my God and my people are made of the same cloth the same blood my people showed up in my vision and I said oh God show me how to make a way—

Grief Interlude III

These days, I live in photographs and little strips of memory. Once, I took you to New York City when I won the—then—biggest award of my life. Now, although I've won one bigger it seems like so much less without you there to ask *where's my share*? You loved that joke. I remember how scared of flying you were—you, the giant of our family, the unbreakable wall around us keeping every bad thing out. I remember the tiny plane, and how I became your comfort. The way your eyes watched for every bump in flight. I remember getting lost in Central Park all afternoon. Taking a photo with Theodore Roosevelt at the Museum of Natural History. The Manhattans you drank with José at the award ceremony. How even the buzz from those drinks couldn't keep you from crying. How proud you were. In the photo on my desk at work, we pretend to be afraid of a dinosaur at the museum. How grateful I am now for this image of you making an exaggerated expression—you always were so stoic in photos normally. Here, you're animated, like you always were in life. Here, you could be ready to launch into a story about what funny thing Mom did last week. You might be able to pivot into a little dance step. I stare and stare and try to replace my last memory of your body with this one. Maybe I can coax a smile onto the face they sewed shut. Some movement into the hands covered by gloves. We bought you new socks for your funeral. If I try, I can make your toes twitch and dance instead of sit idly at the end of a grand casket. If I really wish it so, I can turn that check I wrote to pay for your services into the check we carried, back in New York, gleefully to the bank—I'd never won so much. I can make that check fly right back to that moment, to your hands and mine, to daytime, to hurry, to life—

A Lesson in Distraction/Abstraction—2020 Time Capsule

When I said yes, I meant yes.[1]

The day my cousin died I was deep in preparation for a virtual reading, because the world keeps turning, and I was laughing, moments before we heard the news, which means he was dying or dead while I drank my morning coffee or sang a stupid song or looked at myself in the Zoom window or even while I coughed a meaningless cough and not too long before, I had been sick myself with something I won't name as what I think it was, but it wrecked my body and made my nose bleed like blood was air and my voice got lost somewhere in the phlegm and I still went to work because america has trained me to value only work, not blood—I meant yes, because before that I had wondered what it felt like to not question the open bigotry of liberals and conservatives alike, and I wondered if this last year of tr**p was truly a year to celebrate something like the return of the hidden bigotry of liberals and conservatives alike, and maybe this was before I saw F**K NI**ERS and SHE'S A SASSY NI**ER floating in pixels on the Zoom chat of a program I did online, because this was Our New Normal in These Strange Times—I'd even dressed up for the stream: my black skirt and top, my full fro and red lipstick, even heels because I felt pretty like I hadn't when the man said yes and then no or said I will never make a fool out of you while he, yes, did make a fool out of me, and goodness is this what they mean by when you're with someone you're with everyone they've been with, because even though I'd never had a lover, I did kiss him and he must have also been kissing her and does this mean she and I are now sisters?—I meant yes, and when my cousin died from coronavirus I was laughing at something that probably wasn't even funny, because what is a wasted laugh but a useless clutter of breath, and when we heard the news the world shifted, again, into a purple sort of shape that had been there since the first time I felt pain, when the boy's family let me know Black was forbidden in their white son's kindergarten life, when my grandmas died and my aunts died and my cousins died and I saw death riding them like some cruel rodeo clown and the world told me I really would die alone and maybe my words would outlive me but there's no breath in words and I just want to keep on breathing.

1 The question was: are you afraid to die?

On My Way to the Edmund Pettus Bridge, I Think of My Father

I don't know when will be the last days
of my life. Today, on the road from Montgomery
to Selma, I can't help but think of death. Can't help
but hear its familiar quiet settling down on the bright
green land. There is something in the memory
of protest called fear. Still. I feel it when I remember
the way some men beat the soft pulp
of the marchers' bodies until it was a paste.
I remember the way my skin signifies, sometimes,
chains and the necessity of force. Of death.

Any day could be my last.

I don't know who will be there when it's my time to go,
whether by nature or by force. I wonder
if my father knew it was coming when he died,
if he had a moment to see the sky before
it went black. If he smelled the sweetness
of the breeze as it passed him. I hope he thought of me,
of all of us. I hope he wished us well.
I hope his mother greeted him in heaven,
open arms made of angel wings.

I hope, when it's my time to go, I see him
in an unending garden in the sky,
tending a patch of collards ready to be plucked.
I hope he turns to me with soil on his fingers
and that thinking furrow on his brow.
Maybe, as I leave this earthly realm he'll ask me to help
him pick some greens like we did one Thanksgiving
a lifetime ago. I hope I feel the grip of their green hands.
Their veins full as my soul.

Wellness Exam

The use of a race coefficient in the [eGFR] equation traces back to a study from 1998. It showed that Black people had higher serum (blood) creatinine levels, on average, than whites. Unfortunately, the study had serious limitations. It didn't look at why groups may have differed in their creatinine levels. Plus, it didn't account for the fact that individuals who self-identify as Black are diverse, genetically and biologically. Nonetheless, researchers relied on this flawed science to develop a widely used formula that included a coefficient for Black patients.

Dr. Susanne Nicholas, MD, MPH, PhD, Chair of the UCLA Nephrology Racial and Health Equity Committee

I read the chart because I have a masters degree in Reading Things Well. I see the numbers and their normal ranges. I know I'm a little too heavy. Although my sweetheart might disagree. I am sometimes deficient in iron. I am sometimes full of acid which crowds my chest and makes it get tight—

—and tighter because my dad was overtaken by a tightness in the chest just two years ago. Anxiety is a strange and frightening thing, especially when coupled with a churning moving up, up, up—

I have filled out all the forms. I have marked my age, my gender, my sexual history, my past surgeries, all the vaccines, all the numbers to call if I can't be reached. And yes, you may share my results with my family. I have nothing to hide from them, most of the time. I fill out my allergies—shellfish which makes my throat close up, just like my dad's. And I mark the box for my race. I don't think much of it. I'm always Black and gladly so. One never knows what kind of training the form-makers had. Maybe they've heard of unconscious bias. Maybe they've only heard the Star Spangled Banner. When the chart comes in with my blood test results—the doctor is a rushing kind of man, barely giving me time to explain *I've been having a little pain in my chest but I think I pulled something, I think I need to start that pill, I think I need a new acid reflux prescription because you know I can't swallow pills and the insurance wouldn't cover the chewables the last time*—and then I was off to the lab to get a few vials of blood taken. But the chart. The chart says there's a special calculation to estimate the function of my kidneys because I'm Black. And gladly so. There's a whole other row for our results. This feels like a "colored" sign. Or those false phrenology charts. Or the way I'll probably die on the birthing table. Dr. Sims said it was my fault, my baby's fault. Or the absence of pain in a Black woman's body, they say. Is this like Thomas Jefferson saying we can't reason and we smell real bad? I look it up. This formula is made to account for our so-called naturally higher muscle mass. Higher than what other person, I wonder. How does this formula know my name? And how is the whole rest of humanity good enough for the regular calculation? Does my kidney know it's Black?

African American Literature I

she's crazy / they said / *she's so crazy and you don't learn anything*
richard wright alice walker frantz fanon ralph ellison — nothings
in disguise as somethings
look at her hair / look how it sticks out / look how she dresses / look look look
what did I see but myself in her? fro picked out and loud, fabrics
draped like regal rags
she's too old to teach us / she's senile / she doesn't know what she's doing
in this world, even the phd doesn't equal proficiency —
black modifies scholar
why do we even have to take this class? / I'd rather take shakespeare / milton / someone important
I exist I exist I exist I exist even though the universe says *no* in
iambic pentameter
I said:
I said:
finally, I said: I am learning / she is brilliant / just learn, stop resisting / these books these stories
are mine
you only get A's because you're black / you only get A's because you're black
in this world, even an honors designation doesn't equal proficiency
/ black modifies student

sometimes even I doubted you

who was I to say you were wrong, who were any of us?

didn't we see that the gleam in your eye was not eccentricity, senility, but the very last drop /

of your hope?

Conflict/War

for Gaza, for the Trail of Tears, for Jim Crow and slavery, for the far reaches of colonialism and its violent scythe

This is a brutal place. We blame the dead for their dying. We train our eyes to make their bodies grow to monstrous girth. We say their blood is a necessary sacrifice. Or worse, we forget their blood. The pumping that made them move. The breath that caught before the air filled with shrapnel. Who can help? I stare into the void of my cell phone and search for truth. I stare into the void of my own soul and search for truth. I stare into the void of the governing body and find a void. There is no truth without blood. There is no blood in a constitution. There is no blood in a marbled hall. There is no blood in the gavel which strikes to signal another bill—also bloodless—passed against all the blood just trying to stay within our bodies, trying to do its job. This place is brutal by tradition. Remember discovery and the murders necessary for making a whole new world? Remember Oklahoma. Remember Alabama. Even across the wide sea, the murders we sanction with money, the tanks all filled with fire. The miles and miles of blood. Some of us say *the children, the children.* How do we tell a child her innocence is meaningless? Her blood irrelevant to the bloodless powers that bleed the world? Her blood only a messy inconvenience spilled to fill unfillable hands? Her blood, my blood, all for sale.

Watcher Woman, or, Upon Seeing A Grown White Man Look A Black Girl Up and Down As She Passed By on a Birmingham Street

a golden shovel after Lucille Clifton

I've got my eyes on you. Listen,
I'm a warrior woman, I'm a watcher woman
looking at you look at my children as they pass you
by. Oh you thought no one was checking for a
black girl. Ha! Wonder
who told you
that? Must have been a
conquering man. A murderer of an ancient city
who said: who will care what becomes of
these people we steal? Who will answer for a
Black woman?
I will. I'm watching you.

Don't matter if you got
a degree, a badge, a title, some land, a
whole geography
of
your
own—
I will listen
every time you breathe the wrong way. Every time somebody
looking like me feels like they need
help, like they need a
hero. Ain't nowhere on the map
you can go to
escape my eyes. Please understand—

I'm onto you.

Been on since somebody
came around in 1492 talking about "I need
directions,
we were trying to go to
India." Move
out the way. No room for more conquering around
here. No room for you,
listen, no
room for you in any Black woman,
no room for you
nowhere. Not
even in this country. This street. This body. You are a
noplace
anonymous
man. I saw you looking wrong at a Black girl
as she passed by, and mister,
I got a problem with
that. I'm making this
my problem, buddy. Make sure your hands
don't act on
the plans your eyes make. I'm watching you.

I'll watch and watch around the
whole bloody world until I got
my eye on anyone making plans for pain,
anyone claiming us as his,
anyone with a reaping hook for hands.
Like Jesus on the sparrow, my eye is fixed on
you. On any Dr. Sims, Dr. Death, Mister Man who sees us as some
playground, some discardable skin. I do give a damn

about a Black girl's body.

Masks

What you might not
know is that Columbus
brought diseases to the
so-called new world.

In Hispaniola, the plagues he brought killed 95% of those who lived there first. Plagues like typhus, small and chicken pox, malaria, greed, the snaking sick of manifest that fueled the genocide we call discovery.

There are plagues
we can see and
some we don't.

Not every ailment boils into a glowing pustule. Sometimes, the rot floats, undetectably, through a hand as it signs a bill to law, through a knee as it mounts a pulsing neck, over a belligerent tongue.

Two nights ago I wanted to go home. The airport, empty and silent, was all that stood between me and my bed. Then, almost midnight, and not much there but the plane which brought us from Atlanta and the hot breath of after dark.

At first, I did not hear you speaking to me—what made me turn to you, shake my head *no* to your question about what party I supported? What made me stand and watch you tilt

—a human pinball machine—

with something like excitement? Maybe you smelled fresh blood or the way my hands have never made a fist. *Do you believe in the mask*? You asked me like you really wanted to know, but soon those eyes of yours kept drilling down. Your tone turned sharp. I wonder if you yell at your children that way.

If your mother would be proud to see you screaming at a woman you don't know.

Did you, some airport
arrivals Columbus, see my
body as a waiting feast?

My mask can deflect droplets and maybe even this virus which killed my cousin and millions more.

My mask can conceal my grin when a student makes a joke I shouldn't laugh at.

My mask helps me take deep breaths on the planes I frequent
and fear.

By now, you're telling me how shunned I should be, you're telling me how you obey the 45th american president. You're almost laughing with delight as I turn to you with shock, confusion, anger, and yes, hurt. There is still something in me called a heart, although yours is coated in a cloud of ash, or poison, or maybe one of those many plagues from sea to shining sea.

And your mouth froths—an unclean ocean, and I wonder if there is anything but decay on the other side of its gape and gnarl.

But I am not a conquistador.
I am not a colonizer.

I do not want to plumb
your depths.
Your country can burn
all on its own.

Grief Pantoum

The road home is supposed to bring comfort, but now all I see are the cracks, the blur it all became behind tears on my way to the hospital that April. Now all I see are the cracks: my father staring, bleakly, at the backyard garden; the loudness of the road on my way to the hospital that April; the faint and final smile on his face, now dead. Mom says my father stared, bleakly, at the backyard garden some days before he died. *I want it to look and smell like heaven*, he said. A faint and final smile. His face, now dead, a constant, horrid bell. A frightful palpitation. I want to see Heaven. He said, *I may not come home* when he first took the firehouse job decades ago. All those sirens—a constant, horrid bell. Was he ready for the frightful palpitation, the ache in his chest that was his last and biggest pain? He will never come home. The world is a blur behind tears, an ache in my chest, my biggest pain. The road home brings me no more comfort.

Grief Interlude IV

A socket wrench. A tail light bulb. A screw.
The ringing red blare of a fire truck
when I need to know you're there. When this new
version of you reminds me it's not luck
that we find everything we need, all tools
appear when we, exhausted, call your name
into the broken treadmill, the black spool
of tire losing air. You are the same
in death as in life; you fix everything.
You provide. You, spine of our family
still show up in spirit, soul, you still bring
us comfort, guidance, proof of God's beauty.
Although we're unassembled by your death,
you build us back. You whisper without breath.

It All Begins Here

for ASFA class of 2022

Right now, each breath moves you toward an unwritten future—your body and your mind are unsure machines. Right now, your fingers can barely hold the dreaming in, the questions in, and even the fear—what lives beyond this moment, the warm familiarity of this time spent guarded by parents, school, home, guarded by the far-awayness of *tomorrow*. But don't you know that tomorrow is just another name for new mercy, for blossoming, for the chance to make fresh light? Look at your hands—possibility spills out. From your heart, a moonglow and sunrise. Each breath moves you toward a future, and look, even your breathing decorates the air.

I Know I Feel it, But If I Told You That

I'd have to also tell you that I love the rectangle of air
between your index finger and thumb
when you really have a point to make, nerding out
on Black literature and what america means and how language works,
on the words you drop in conversation or in a text thread
that you know, and that sometimes I know, too,
and sometimes I have to look up,
and I hope you don't think less of me for it.
I love the mystery of your vocabulary. The expansive way it sprawls.
I'd also have to tell you that the way you sing out loud
no matter the time of day or night, no matter where we are
makes me feel like there's maybe a way to build joy out of breath alone.
I'd have to tell you that my breaths feel like love now, too.
I'd have to tell you that the taste of morning on your lips
is sweet as childhood Kool-Aid and as fresh
as its shimmy over ice. I'd have to tell you I can't stop drinking it.
I'd have to tell you that just to be near you,
just there in the room even if there's football on,
because there's always football on—and I hate football—
that that nearness feels like the exhale
Whitney Houston and Loretta Devine and Angela Bassett
and even Lela Rochon yelling at Bubba from Forrest Gump
off her balcony
wanted to feel. I can stretch into our love.

I'd have to tell you that what I feel is bright and loud
even in this endless chamber of grief. I wish my dad could meet you.
I wish I could meet yours.

I want to tell you that I love you
but then I'd have to say it all.

Grief Interlude V

At the quiktrip I see a middle-aged Black man with a bag full of gas station snacks. Salty, certainly. Cholesterol be damned. As he gets into his truck, I think, *that should be you.* You wanted another truck soon, you told us not too long before you died. You'd had one before—I don't remember why you traded it in. Probably to buy one for us—you always put us first. I don't know who cleaned out your Fire Chief Truck after everything. I don't know who's driving it now. I think of the sound of your palm against the steering wheel as it moved in your hands. The swish that signaled life. I see this man at the gas station and I think it should be you. When my mom looks toward the sun I think, *she should be looking at you.* Her smile, your glow. When I relish in the comfort of my love, a man you'll never meet, I don't know how she faces any day without you. The pain is too big. My joy feels so temporary. But still worth it, like you—

Ida Mae, Queen of Joy

after RaMell Moss

This is no lost son's funeral.
This is no Sunday jubilee. This
is no cause to wonder
if heaven is a place where freedom really
stretches out flat and yielding on its back.
This is a bit of sun stinging the star in my eye,
the sweat from a hot Alabama afternoon pooling,
dripping. A tear re-entering its tomb.

This is *my good wig*.

This is a day to wear it and not even clip it down,
because this is a delicate day.
No running from an angry gnarl and siren,
not today. And these pantyhose,
the polyester skin across my righteous knee
will only kneel before Jesus himself,
but he surely wouldn't ask me that. Not today,
when He rolled out this cloudless sky,
so smooth I would spread it on a Saltine
and take it in my mouth—
the prayer it would make on my tongue.
Everybody knows all of us
whose first names are punctuated by Mae
know Jesus personally—right down to our cuticles.
Right down to the sharpest shadow he casts behind us—
so black, so deep, it shows the Beginning,
before "before." It is the pause before God made the world.
It is the shine on my Sunday shoes
the holy guarantee of hard candy in my pocketbook.

And it's joy, and it's mine,
and it's hallelujah, mine, mine, mine.

Grief Interlude VI

When I met my love I wondered what you would say.
But you are beyond saying.

Lullaby For the Grieving

at the Sipsey River

make small steps.
in this wild place
there are signs of life
everywhere.
sharp spaces, too:
the slip of a rain-glazed rock
against my searching feet.
small steps, like prayers—
each one a hope exhaled
into the trees. please,
let me enter. please, let me
leave whole.
there are, too, the tiny sounds
of faraway birds. the safety
in their promise of song.
the puddle forming, finally,
after summer rain.
the golden butterfly
against the cave-dark.
maybe there are angels here, too—
what else can i call the crown of light
atop the leaves?
what else can i call
my footsteps forward,
small, small, sure?

Grief

In my dreams, my father has wisdom
of living beyond the grave.
He can laugh, walk, run.
He can wield anger.
He can shed tears.

Last night, he threw a baseball in the air,
marveled at its constant return.
His joy was boyish.
His eyes were bright and small above his smile.

I don't know
if I should think about returning,
how his face keeps showing up in mine.
The way my eyes shrink in my own joy.

He even plays tricks in my dreams.
Makes jokes that make me scold him.
What luxury to be mad
at him in a dream—
in waking life, I only feel longing. The empty days to fill.
I would never be angry again
if he walked through any door.

The ball goes up and falls down.
I watch and marvel at his beauty in an open field.
I return to my life and he is gone.

Love and Happiness

an elegy for Daphne Bowman Powell

Let's stay in those weekday mornings
while we settled into work, when the day had just begun
and there were letters to write,
scholarship data ready for report,
the errands I'd soon run in the old state car—

let's stay in those mornings
when we were already burrowed
in the white glow of our screens, and then,
a ripple of laughter peels from your lips
and I look to see a smile lingering there.

Let's stay in the moment where you tell me a story,
a funny anecdote that happened over the weekend
or in an article you'd just read,
and this time, let me stay in that morning you turned to me
and played "Love and Happiness" by Al Green,
loud and clear from your desktop computer
with the whole office working quietly down the hall,

and let's stay in the moment your eyes brightened
as you started to dance to the guitar's knowing plucks,
and let's stay, friend, in that moment
where we sang together,
and you taught me that there was always room for joy,
even in the middle of a workweek,
even in an office full of numbers needing counting
and meetings needing to be met—

there is room for joy in Al Green's moan for love
and your voice rising to meet his,
in your invitation for me to join the song,
to find my own spirit sailing to the tune,
to laugh and make life sweeter, always.

Grief Interlude VII

I haven't been myself for three years.
I don't know who's walking in my skin.
More often than not, I wake up in tears.

Yesterday, I was angry if anyone was near,
but I also didn't want to be alone. I live in contradiction.
I haven't been myself for three years.

I used to sing each morning. My voice was clear.
Now, it rasps from sickness or grief. My song is sullen.
More often than not, I wake up in tears.

My joy is different. Laughter laced with fear—
how soon will I look death in its eyes again?
I haven't been myself for three years.

I dream and dream that you'll reappear,
you'll tell me it was all pretend.
More often than not, I wake up in tears,

and even awake, I can't unsee the truth. There's no repair
for your stillness in the casket. The grieving without end.
I haven't been myself for three years.
More often, forever, I'll wake up in tears.

On Entering the New Year Without My Father

a golden shovel after Lucille Clifton

this morning, when my breath catches
and the tears come, I see the
year ahead unfolding without him. this sun
is one he won't feel, save the rays that spread and
burn on our backs at his grave. what keeps
us here after such loss? most
might be quick to say God, and of
course it's Him,
but God loved my dad, too. before
his death, I could have gobbled the
world up like a ball of bubblegum. sleep came in the evening
without the dark quick panic that
daggers me, heart first. surely,
someday, I'll awake to these empty days, certain that things will
look more like light, that the answers to my prayers will come.

Snow Poem

for Dad

This is not a poem about snow. No,
not even about winter or ice, flakes
making pretty shapes, geometric glow.
Instead, it's about the chill your death makes

over and again in my bones. My heart.
Instead, this is about the way you laughed
when you made bad jokes. The way you made art
with no lessons—yours a natural craft

from your mind and hands alone. The garden,
the Christmas village, the portraits hanging
in our foyer, the way you cooked, sharpened
your knife. Your life's example said: making

a promise is a sacred, solid vow.
Now you're gone. I wonder where you are now.

—

Now you're gone. I wonder where you are now.
Sometimes I lose a detail of your face,
a shade of your voice, the print of your brow.
You float away. You leave no earthly trace.

Sometimes I see you outside tending plants.
Your phantom makes illusions in the yard:
salting a slab of ribs, making fire dance
in the mouth of the grill, the charcoal charred.

Mom says she met you in a dream, just days
after you left. You said you had your wings.
Your earthly wish to be a big bird made
real by God in Heaven. Does flight now bring

you back? I know I feel you in the wind.
I know your love for us can never end.

—

I know your love for us can never end.
I know I'm still your daughter after death.
I know your love for us can never end.
I know I'm still your daughter after death.

I know your love for us can never end.
I know I'm still your daughter after death.
I know your love for us can never end.
I know I'm still your daughter after death.

I know your love for us can never end.
I know I'm still your daughter after death.
I know your love for us can never end.
I know I'm still your daughter after death.

But that knowing doesn't stop brutal time.
Days move on. We stay in the day you died.

—

Days move on. We stay in the day you died—
I think back to those hours before I knew
for sure. When the world still made sense. I cried
the whole way home to take mom there to you,

praying all the while that you'd be okay.
But the road already knew. The clouds too.
My face a mess, my screams, my disarray.
Had I resigned myself then to the truth?

I can't unsee myself becoming old
beyond my years. Putting on a strong mask
when I saw you, finally, still and cold
on the hospital slab. I still can't grasp

that reality. My body rejects
that sight. Your body an unreal object.

—

That sight, your body an unreal object,
I held Mom's body, crumpled by her grief.
For the first time, you weren't there to protect
us. You weren't there to give our hearts relief.

Months before, I remember your sharp tone
on the phone: *get in the damn crawlspace now*!
As you looked in your rearview, a cyclone
formed in the sky. Unpredicted threat, how

did my dad protect us from it when all
around us, just a street over, complete
destruction? Lives lost and branches fallen
from the force of wind. The scattered debris.

And yet, we still felt safe. That's what you were
to us. Maybe, that's still what you are.

—

To us, maybe that is still what you are,
the fence to hold things out and keep us in.
When I'm scared, I feel you saying *don't fear*,
even now, when my faith in life is thin,

you're in the rosebud, softly seeking light,
in the wrenches and screwdrivers we use
to fix the house, its walls your skin, your might.
The redbird's song, a sound I can't confuse

for anything but your spirit singing.
I thank God for that song. For the gentle
way you smile through the leafy canopy
of trees filtering sunlight's miracle.

Dad, I still can't believe it's been three years.
I know now that grief never disappears.

—

I know now that grief never disappears.
When I saw you stare out over the graves
of your mother, granny, sisters, brothers,
the fog in your eyes should have said, grief leaves

no room for anything but grief. It lifts
from time to time, but never forever.
Once, you said you felt torn between two worlds:
most of my people are already there,

already in the beyond. What footing
is there between heaven and earth? Between
memory and memories-yet-made? Bring
back the balance of a complete family—

all of us here, alive. Bring back a past
we fear and love. Love is too good to last.

—

We fear and love. Love is too good to last,
but we do it anyway. You showed us
how to make it. How it spreads. It could cast
our hardships away, worries into dust.

That love remains. So does the shape of you
in the corners of my eyes. My stubborn
streak which rears up more now. You are there, too,
when I learn to birth new love on my own.

The blueprint was always there—you and Mom
shaped light around each other, showing us
that love can be safety, can be the calm
before all that storms, in and around us.

Your love is a shield no man can threaten.
Every night I pray you're safe in Heaven.

—

Every night I pray you're safe in Heaven.
Every day I search for my memories.
Who were you when you were so much less than
dead, when you were Dad, fueling our joy-cries

of laughter as you played tickle monster,
your funk music blasting: "Atomic Dog"
and Earth, Wind, and Fire. Saltine crackers
and hoghead cheese—it's all a distant fog

now, but it comforts me still. The music
of your singing voice, the odd way you danced—
badly, but with feeling. This is the trick
of time—joy blinds us, tragically entranced.

And when time stops the hearts of those we love,
we fight our faith, we plead to God above.

—

We fight our faith, we plead to God above
for answers that never belonged to us.
God knew us first. He was the giver of
our birth and our death. But now, I still fuss

with the *what ifs* and all the *should have dones,*
the laughs unlaughed, the precious time unspent,
the way this place leaves Black people undone,
the constant nagging threat of mortgage, rent,

four children's college debt all paid in full,
two jobs at least, the house always repaired,
the garden planted, the cookouts, the lull
of this life he provided us, the care

we can't repay. How sheltered we all were.
I never knew life could be a sad blur.

—

I never knew life could be a sad blur.
My privileged, happy thirty years. My dad,
the hero of everything. It occurs
to me now how much he carried. How bad

the darkness was in his own childhood past,
The terrors he faced at home and outside,
the stories he told us briefly. The glass
of his eyes cloudy with memory. I

know there was so much more he never told.
So much he overcame in his short life.
I'm proud of who he was. I walk boldly
in his shadow. I ask the afterlife:

will you take care of him since we cannot?
I hope his soul escaped the casket's rot.

—

I hope his soul escaped the casket's rot,
I hope his pain was brief before he died,
What was his life's last meal? A shining pot
of pinto beans, a Southern chicken fry?

I hope he'd made his peace before the pain,
that he and God had talked and understood
each other. That God made balm for the strain
in my father's failing heart. That he could

fly up from his body before it stopped,
that Heaven opened immediately,
that eternal joy and gladness unlocked
the golden gates for him. I hope he's free.

I hope he chooses to look down on us.
I hope, one day, my heart can mend, adjust.

—

I hope. One day my heart can mend, adjust
to this new life. One day it breaks anew.
Sometimes I lose his voice. I cannot trust
my memory to hold him there. I grew

accustomed to his body bouncing back
from any kind of ailment through the years.
He was a man. Now, I can see the cracks
in my own façade—humanity rears

its head now to show my lack. What I need
is constant, and the wants are luxury.
Thirty years I was untouched by death's greed—
I should be grateful it took less from me.

My selfish heart must learn to love what was—
not everyone can know a father's love.

—

Not everyone can know a father's love,
God gave me so much in your warm embrace,
in your thoughtfulness, putting us above
all else. Thank you. No one can take your place.

No one can call me Ash Berry or rough
my hair. No one can call my big head big
or advise me to be mentally tough.
No one can feed me the head of a pig

made into sousemeat to spread on crackers
but you. No one can make me write of snow.
I hope this poem can somehow measure
up to all you showed me. All I now know.

I'll love you always, Donald Lewis Jones,
my dad, my hero, fire in my bones.

—

Now you're gone. I wonder where you are now.
I know your love for us can never end.
Days move on. We stay in the day you died:
that sight, your body an unreal object.
To us, maybe, that is still what you are.
I know now that grief never disappears.
We fear and love. Love is too good to last.
Every night I pray you're safe in Heaven.
We fight our faith, we plead to God above.
I never knew life could be a sad blur.
I hope your soul escaped the casket's rot,
I hope, one day, my heart can mend, adjust.
Not everyone can know a father's love—
my dad, my hero, fire in my bones.

Imagine Us, In Love With the World

I want to tell you a story about love. About peace.

Some days, long before today, I would wake
to hear the wind rustling my parents' voices
as they sipped coffee and settled into the morning
of their love.

I could hear the redbirds draw close
to carefully puncture the air with their calls.
The soft movement of houseclothes
against the metal patio chairs.
The intake of coffee like a suction—
the pause as they let it steam down their throats.
The sun stretching against the backyard plants.

Days like these, all I did was stand and wait.
I'd listen. What could I learn there in the stillness?
What meditation in making my breath
shallow so my parents could not hear it,
so their seclusion remained intact,
so I could hear them exist without my imposition,
without the day begging for attention,
its constant wail of need.

In that stillness, that listening, I understood
how precious, how delicate it is to be alive,
to carry air and a heartbeat. To relax against your bones.
I could ease into that tranquility
and find light there. I could find a place
for my soul to rest and be at peace.

These days, I cling to that memory,
the truth of that gentle moment

and its harmony. These days, I hold that feeling
against the wound my living makes—
against the sharp, swift scythe of loved ones lost,
of politics making fiction into fact,
against the rattle of danger
exploding from an angry barrel,
aimed at my head, my heart.

When the darkness comes I can close my eyes
and go right back to the morning whispers
over coffee, the sunrise meeting my parents
and the dance of steam from those mugs.
The peace there.
The way that moment is sealed inside me.
The way it protects me still,
coating me in my worthiness,
bathing me in their love.

Acknowledgements

"What It Really Is" – *Sierra Club Magazine*

"I Feel Powerful When" – *Black Imagination 2: Black Powerful*

"Home: Variations" – *Hammer and Hope*

"All God's Children Got Wings" – *The History of White People In America*

"A Meat and Three for the Jubliee" – *Oxford American*

"The Heart" – commissioned and performed for Higher Ground Society's album, *Patchwork Symphony*

"Freedom Sermon, Alabama, USA" – commissioned for and published by Alabama Humanities Alliance

"A Map of The Capitol – Montgomery, USA" – MONUMENTS exhibit, *Salvation South*

"When You Ask Me From Where My Help Comes" – commissioned by Community Foundation of Greater Birmingham for the International Peace Conference, *Salvation South*

"I Think of You, Alabama" – commissioned by the World Games

"Black, Black, Blue" – commissioned by Erin Leann Mitchell for the Alabama Triennial Exhibition

"A Portrait of Harriet" – commissioned by and performed first with the Alabama School of Fine Arts Music Department, in collaboration with Dr. Rebekah Griffin Greene

"HolyHeadHarriet" – *Poem-A-Day*, January 2025

"A Lesson in Distraction/Abstraction – 2020 Time Capsule" – *Hypertext* Magazine

"On My Way to the Edmund Pettus Bridge, I Think of My Father" – *The Forum* by Phi Kappa Phi

"African American Literature I" – *The Magnitude of Us: An Educator's Guide to Creating Culturally Responsive Classrooms*

"Conflict//War" – *Salvation South*

"Masks" – *Huizache*

"Grief Pantoum" – *Huizache*

"It All Begins Here" – commissioned by Alabama School of Fine Arts

"Ida Mae, Queen of Joy" – commissioned by Jule Collins Smith Museum of Art at Auburn University

"Lullaby for the Grieving" – *You Are Here: Poetry In the Natural World*, Milkweed Editions 2025

"Imagine Us, In Love with the World" – commissioned by International Peace Conference

Ashley M. Jones is the Poet Laureate of Alabama (2022-2026). She is the first person of color and the youngest person to hold this position in its 93 year existence. She holds an MFA in Poetry from Florida International University, and she is the author of *Magic City Gospel*, *dark // thing*, and *Reparations Now!*, which was longlisted for the 2022 PEN/Voelcker Award for Poetry. Jones is the founding director of the Magic City Poetry Festival. She is the Associate Director of the University Honors Program at UAB, and she is part of the Core Faculty of the Converse University Low Residency MFA Program.

PUBLISHING
New & Extraordinary
VOICES FROM THE
AMERICAN SOUTH

HUB CITY PRESS is a non-profit independent press in Spartanburg, SC that publishes well-crafted, high-quality works by new and established authors, with an emphasis on the Southern experience. We are committed to high-caliber novels, short stories, poetry, plays, memoir, and works emphasizing regional culture and history. We are particularly interested in books with a strong sense of place.

Hub City Press is an imprint of the non-profit Hub City Writers Project, founded in 1995 to foster a sense of community through the literary arts. Our metaphor of organization purposely looks backward to the nineteenth century when Spartanburg was known as the "hub city," a place where railroads converged and departed.

RECENT HUB CITY PRESS POETRY

The Girl Who Became a Rabbit • Emilie Menzel

Joy is the Justic We Give Ourselves • J. Drew Lanham

The Last Saturday in America • Ray McManus

El Rey of Gold Teeth • Reyes Ramirez

In the Hands of the River • Lucien Darjeun Meadows

Thresh & Hold • Marlanda Dekine

Reparations Now! • Ashley M. Jones

Sparrow Envy: A Field Guide to Birds and Lesser Beasts • J. Drew Lanham

Cleave • Tiana Nobile

Mustard, Milk, and Gin • Megan Denton Ray

Dusk & Dust • Esteban Rodriguez